INTRODUCTION

Welcome back to FastTrack®!

Hope you enjoyed *Drums 1* and are ready to play some hits. Have you and your friends formed a band? Or do you feel like soloing with the audio? Either way, make sure you're relaxed…it's time to jam!

With the knowledge you already have, you're ready to play all of these eight songs. But it's still important to remember the three Ps: **patience**, **practice** and **pace yourself**.

As with Drums 1, don't try to bite off more than you can chew. If you're tired, take some time off. If you get frustrated, put down your sticks, relax and just listen to the audio. If you forget something, go back and learn it. If you're doing fine, think about charging admission.

CONTENTS

ABOUT THE AUDIO

Again, you get audio with the book! Each song in the book is included on the audio, so you can hear how it sounds and play along when you're ready.

Each audio example is preceded by one measure of "clicks" to indicate the tempo and meter. Pan right to hear the drum part emphasized. Pan left to hear the accompaniment emphasized.

ISBN 978-0-634-00262-5

To access audio visit:
www.halleonard.com/mylibrary

4674-3376-1021-5160

HAL•LEONARD®
CORPORATION
7777 W. BLUEMOUND RD. P.O. BOX 13819 MILWAUKEE, WI 53213

Visit Hal Leonard Online at
www.halleonard.com

LEARN SOMETHING NEW EACH DAY

We know you're eager to play, but first you need to learn a few new things. We'll make it brief — only one page...

Melody and Lyrics

All of the melody lines and lyrics of these great songs (except for "Walk Don't Run" which is an instrumental) are included for your musical pleasure (and benefit). These are shown on an extra musical staff, which we added above your part.

Unfortunately, drummers never play the melody (we can't imagine why not?!), but this added vocal line will help you follow the song more easily as you play your part.

And whether you have a singer in the band or decide to carry the tune yourself, this new staff is your key to adding some vocals to your tunes.

Several of the songs have some interesting little symbols that you must understand before playing. Each of these symbols represents a different type of ending.

Endings

1st and 2nd Endings

You know these from Drums 1 (the brackets with numbers):

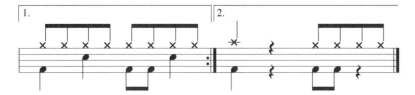

D.S. al Coda

When you see these words, go back and repeat from this symbol: 𝄋

Play until you see the words "To Coda" then skip to the Coda, indicated by this symbol: ⊕

Now just finish the song.

That's about it! Enjoy the music...

Evil Ways

Words and Music by Sonny Henry

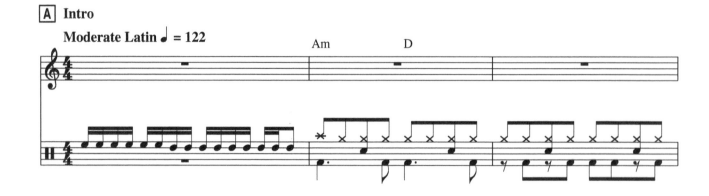

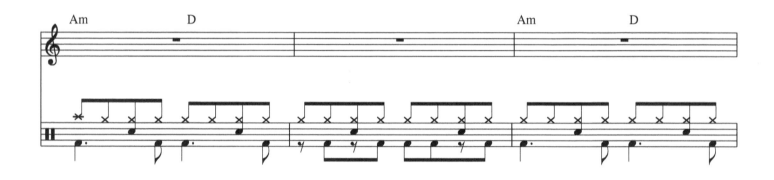

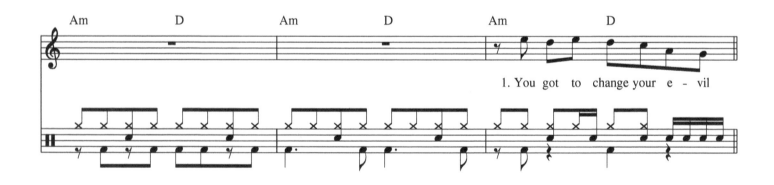

change.

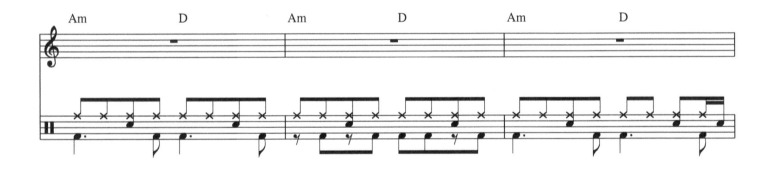

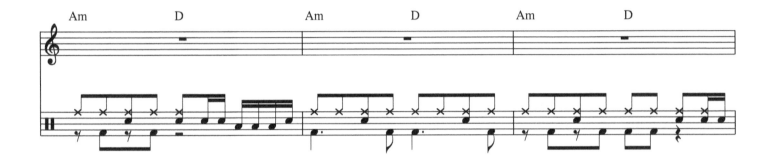

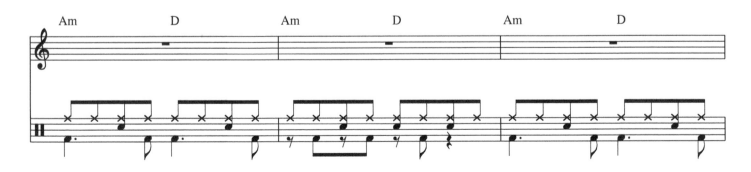

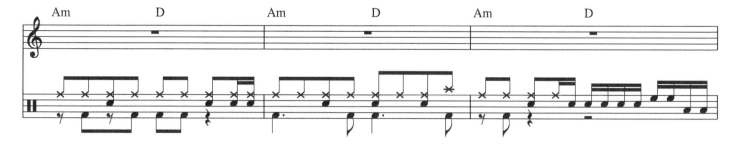

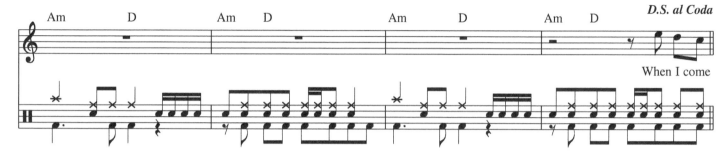

D.S. al Coda

When I come

⊕ *Coda*

E7

on.   Yeah, yeah, yeah. _____

D Outro-Guitar Solo

_____ Hey, hey.

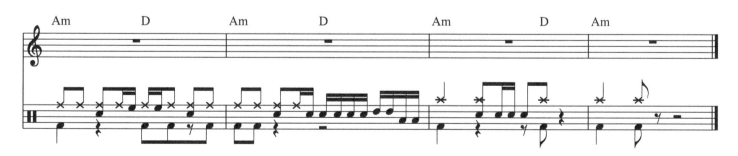

7

Gimme Some Lovin'

Words and Music by Spencer Davis, Muff Winwood and Steve Winwood

A Intro

Moderately Fast ♩ = 152

B Interlude

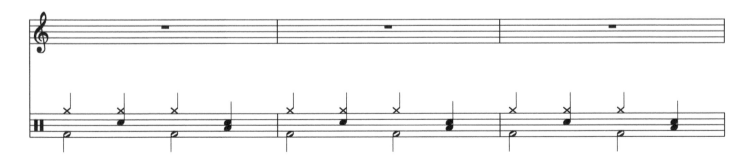

Gloria

Words and Music by Van Morrison

Lord. She makes me feel al - right. And her name is G,

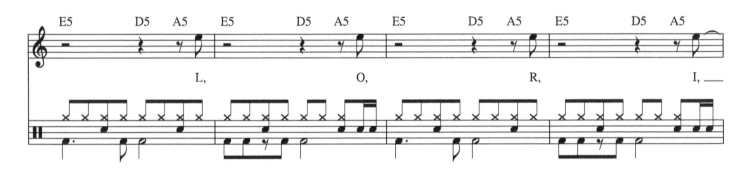

L, O, R, I, ___

𝄋

C Chorus

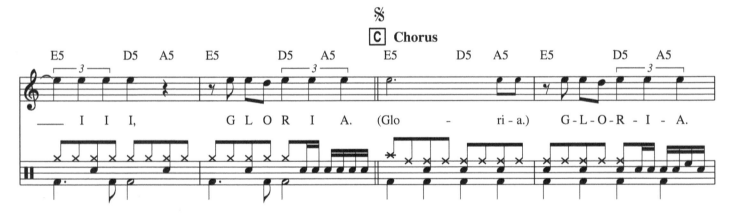

___ I I I, G L O R I A. (Glo - ri-a.) G-L-O-R-I-A.

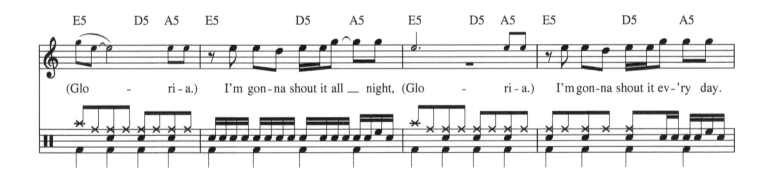

(Glo - ri-a.) I'm gon-na shout it all ___ night, (Glo - ri-a.) I'm gon-na shout it ev-'ry day.

To Coda ⊕

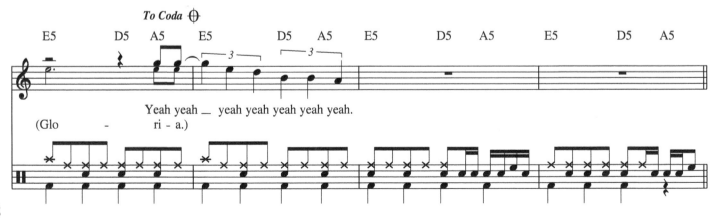

Yeah yeah ___ yeah yeah yeah yeah yeah.
(Glo - ri-a.)

◆4 Have I Told You Lately

Words and Music by Van Morrison

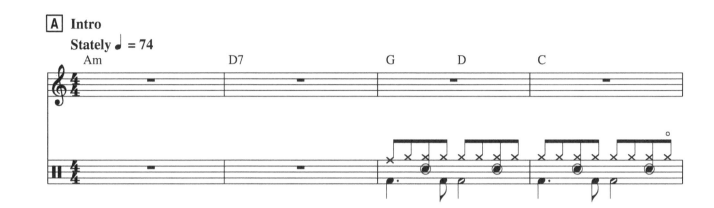

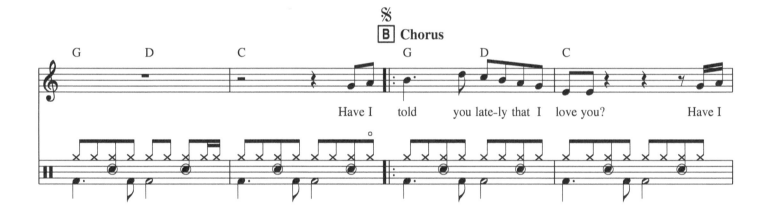

Have I told you late-ly that I love you? Have I

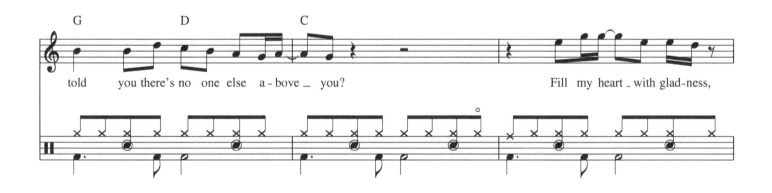

told you there's no one else a-bove _ you? Fill my heart _ with glad-ness,

take a-way all _ my sad-ness, ease my trou-bles that's _ what you do. For the

we should give thanks and pray ___ to the one, _ to the one. _ Have I

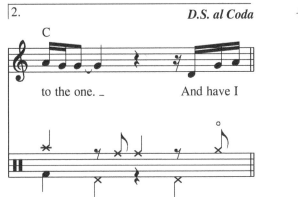

to the one. _ And have I

D.S. al Coda

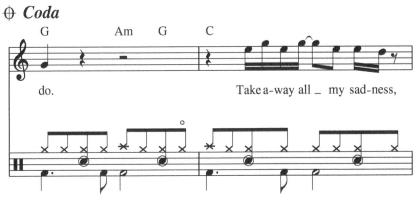

Coda

do. Take a-way all _ my sad-ness,

Fill my life with glad-ness, ease my trou-bles that's _ what you do.

Take a-way all _ my sad-ness, fill my heart with glad-ness, ease my trou-bles that's _ what you do. ___

rit.

Jailhouse Rock

Words and Music by Jerry Leiber and Mike Stoller

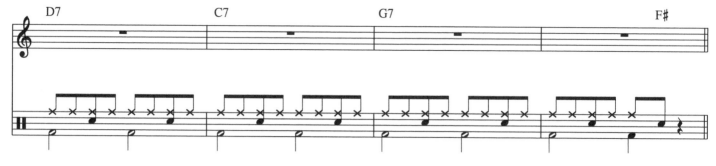

Additional Lyrics

3. Number Forty-seven said to number Three:
   "You're the cutest jailbird I ever did see.
   I sure would be delighted with your company.
   Come on and do the Jailhouse Rock with me."

4. The sad sack was a-sittin' on a block of stone,
   Way over in a corner weeping all alone.
   The warden said: "Hey, Buddy, don't you be no square,
   If you can't find a partner, use a wooden chair!"

(optional)

5. Shifty Henry said to Bugs: "For heaven's sake.
   No one's lookin', now's our chance to make a break."
   Bugsy turned to Shifty and he said, "Nix, nix;
   I wanna stick around a while and get my kicks."

6 Time Is on My Side

Words and Music by Jerry Ragovoy

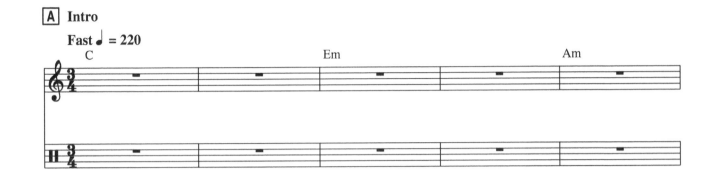

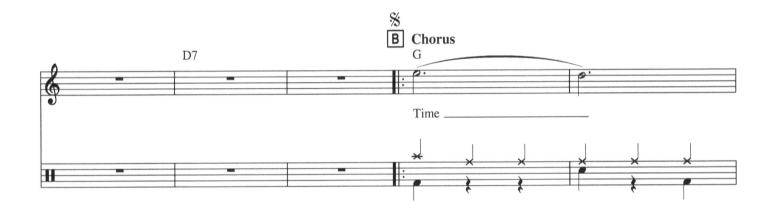

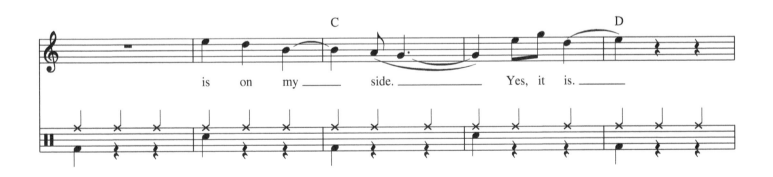

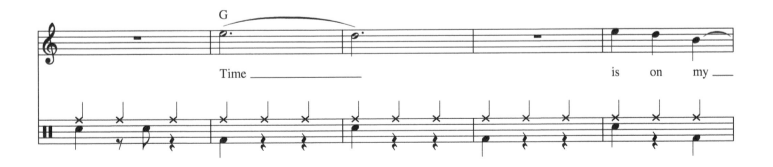

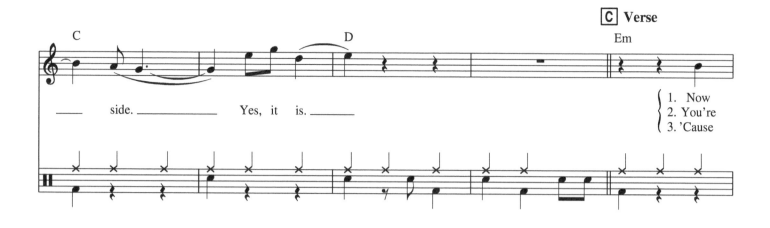

side. _____ Yes, it is. _____

1. Now
2. You're
3. 'Cause

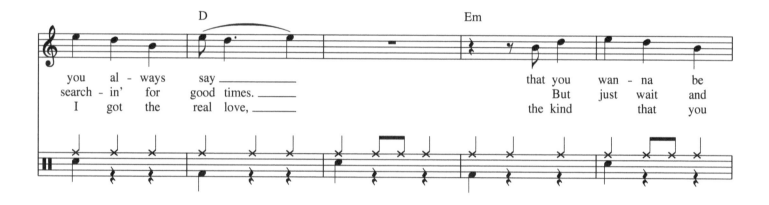

you al - ways say _____ that you wan - na be
search - in' for good times. _____ But just wait and
I got the real love, _____ the kind that you

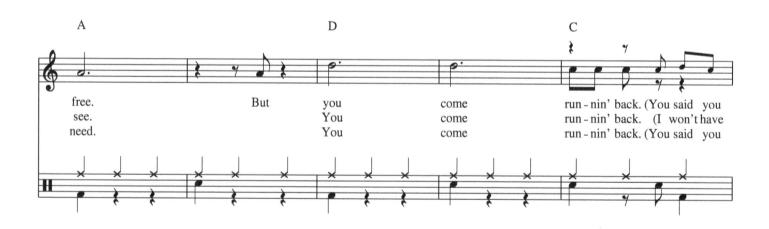

free. But you come run - nin' back. (You said you
see. You come run - nin' back. (I won't have
need. You come run - nin' back. (You said you

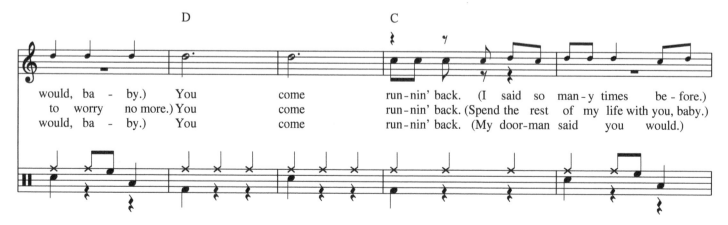

would, ba - by.) You come run - nin' back. (I said so man - y times be - fore.)
to worry no more.) You come run - nin' back. (Spend the rest of my life with you, baby.)
would, ba - by.) You come run - nin' back. (My door - man said you would.)

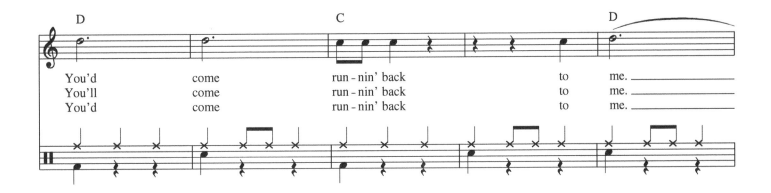

You'd come run-nin' back to me. _____
You'll come run-nin' back to me. _____
You'd come run-nin' back to me. _____

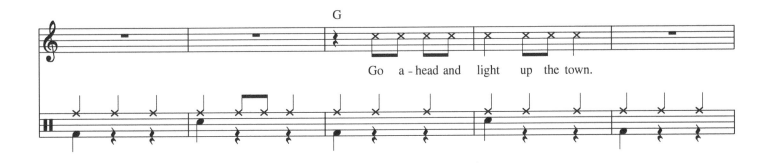

To Coda ⊕

D **Bridge**

Oh, _
Yes, _

Go a-head.

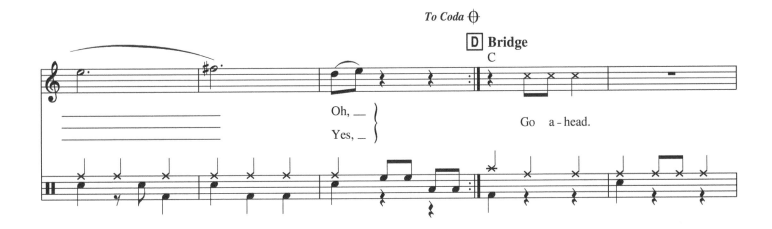

Go a-head and light up the town.

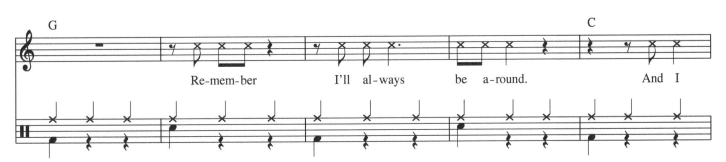

And, ba-by, do ev-'ry-thing your heart de-sires.

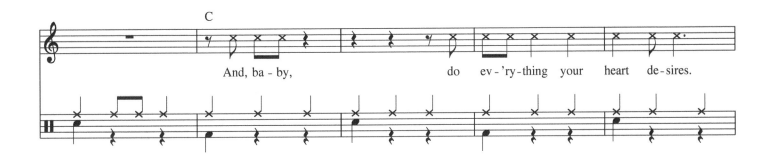

Re-mem-ber I'll al-ways be a-round. And I

7 Twist and Shout

Words and Music by Bert Russell and Phil Medley

A Intro

Moderate Rock 'n' Roll ♩ = 127

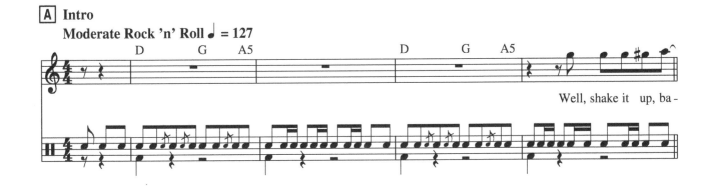

Well, shake it up, ba-

B Chorus

-by, _ now. (Shake it up, ba - by.) Twist and shout. _ (Twist and shout. _

_)C'm-on _ c'm-on _ c'm-on _ c'm-on, ba - by, _ now.   C'm-on and work it on out. _
(C'm-on, ba - by.)

C Verse

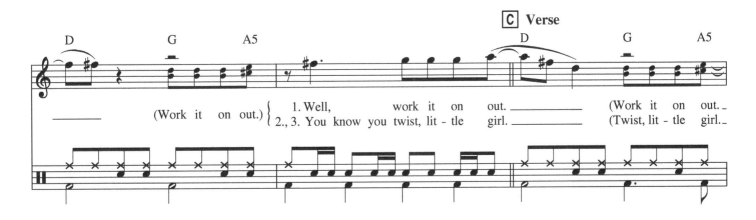

_ (Work it on out.) 1. Well, work it on out. _ (Work it on out. _
2., 3. You know you twist, lit - tle girl. _ (Twist, lit - tle girl. _

Ah. _____ Ah. Whoa yeah. _ Ba-

⊕ *Coda*

D   G   A5

Well, shake it, shake it, shake it, ba - by, _ now.   Well, shake it, shake it, shake it,
                    (Shake it up, ba - by.)

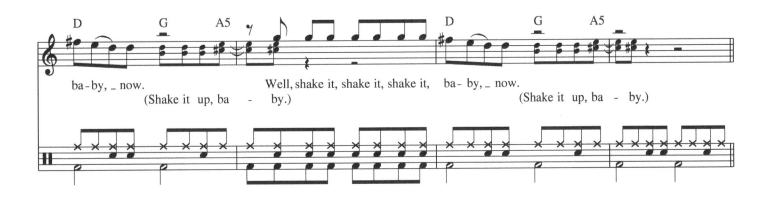

D   G   A5   D   G   A5

ba - by, _ now.   Well, shake it, shake it, shake it, ba - by, _ now.
(Shake it up, ba - by.)   (Shake it up, ba - by.)

F Outro

A5   D

Ah. _____ Ah. _____ Ah. _____ Ah.

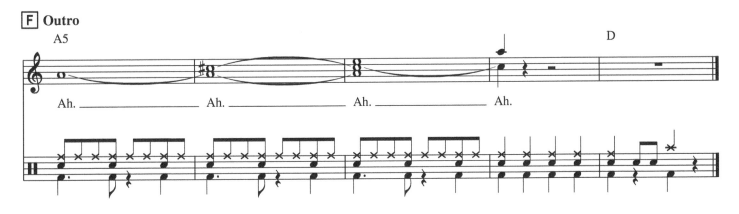

Walk Don't Run

Words and Music by Johnny Smith

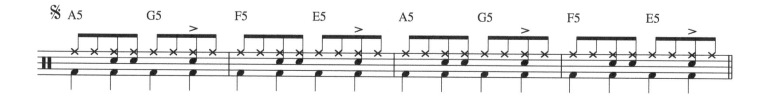

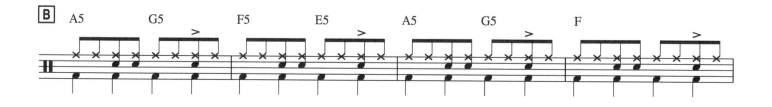

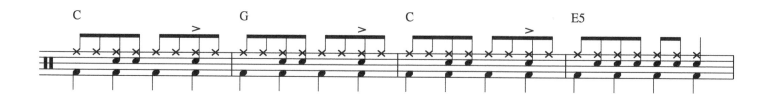

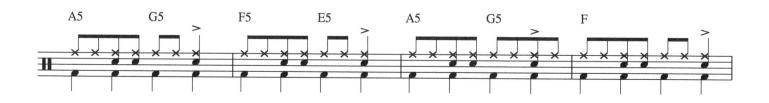

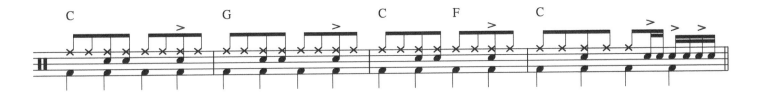

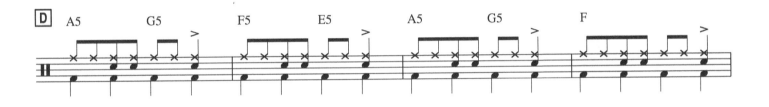

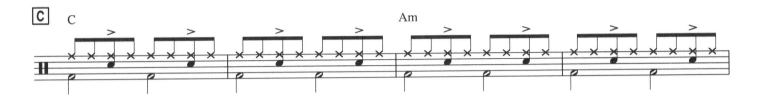

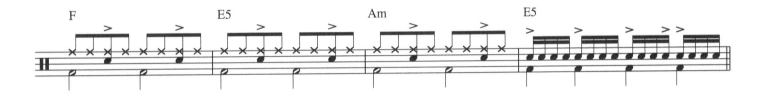

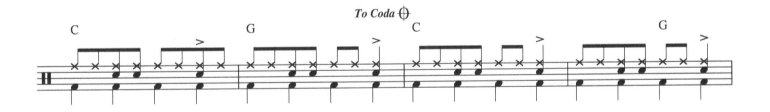

To Coda ⊕

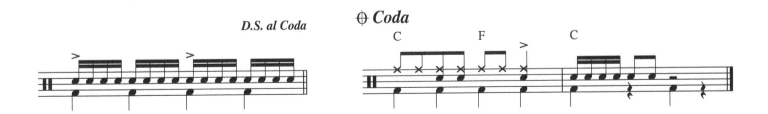

D.S. al Coda

⊕ *Coda*

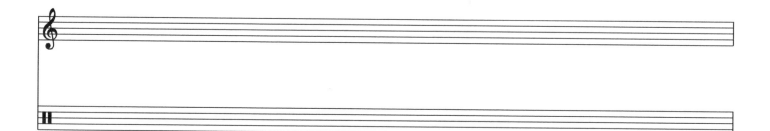

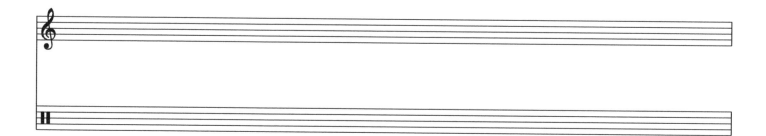

FastTrack is the fastest way for beginners to learn to play the instrument they just bought. **FastTrack** is different from other method books: we've made our book/audio packs user-friendly with plenty of cool songs that make it easy and fun for players to teach themselves. Plus, the last section of the books have the same songs so that students can form a band and jam together. Songbooks for guitar, bass, keyboard and drums are all compatible, and feature eight songs. All packs include great play-along audio with a professional-sounding back-up band.

FastTrack Bass

by Blake Neely & Jeff Schroedl

Level 1

00264732	Method Book/Online Media	$14.99
00697284	Method Book/Online Audio	$7.99
00696404	Method Book/Online Audio + DVD	$14.99
00697289	Songbook 1/Online Audio	$12.99
00695368	Songbook 2/Online Audio	$12.99
00696440	Rock Songbook with CD	$12.99
00696058	DVD	$7.99

Level 2

00697294	Method Book/Online Audio	$9.99
00697298	Songbook 1/Online Audio	$12.99
00695369	Songbook 2/Online Audio	$12.99

FastTrack Drum

by Blake Neely & Rick Mattingly

Level 1

00264733	Method Book/Online Media	$14.99
00697285	Method Book/Online Audio	$7.99
00696405	Method Book/Online Audio + DVD	$14.99
00697290	Songbook 1/Online Audio	$12.99
00695367	Songbook 2/Online Audio	$12.99
00696441	Rock Songbook with CD	$12.99
00696059	DVD	$7.99

Level 2

00697295	Method Book/Online Audio	$9.99
00697299	Songbook 1/Online Audio	$12.99
00695371	Songbook 2/Online Audio	$12.99

FastTrack Guitar

For Electric or Acoustic Guitar, or Both

by Blake Neely & Jeff Schroedl

Level 1

00264731	Method Book/Online Media	$14.99
00697282	Method Book/Online Audio	$7.99
00696403	Method Book/Online Audio + DVD	$14.99
00697287	Songbook 1/Online Audio	$12.99
00695343	Songbook 2/Online Audio	$12.99
00696438	Rock Songbook with CD	$12.99
00696057	DVD	$7.99

Level 2

00697286	Method Book/Online Audio	$9.99
00697296	Songbook/Online Audio	$14.99

Chords & Scales

00697291	Book/Online Audio	$10.99

FastTrack Keyboard

For Electric Keyboard, Synthesizer or Piano

by Blake Neely & Gary Meisner

Level 1

00264734	Method Book/Online Media	$14.99
00697283	Method Book/Online Audio	$7.99
00696406	Method Book/Online Audio + DVD	$14.99
00697288	Songbook 1/Online Audio	$12.99
00696439	Rock Songbook with CD	$12.99
00696060	DVD	$7.99

Level 2

00697293	Method Book/Online Audio	$9.99

Chords & Scales

00697292	Book/Online Audio	$9.99

FastTrack Harmonica

by Blake Neely & Doug Downing

Level 1

00695407	Method Book/Online Audio	$7.99
00695958	Mini Method Book with CD	$7.95
00820016	Mini Method/CD + Harmonica	$12.99
00695574	Songbook/Online Audio	$12.99

Level 2

00695889	Method Book/Online Audio	$9.99
00695891	Songbook with CD	$12.99

FastTrack Lead Singer

by Blake Neely

Level 1

00695408	Method Book/Online Audio	$7.99
00695410	Songbook/Online Audio	$14.99

Level 2

00695890	Method Book/Online Audio	$9.95
00695892	Songbook with CD	$12.95

FastTrack Saxophone

by Blake Neely

Level 1

00695241	Method Book/Online Audio	$7.99
00695409	Songbook/Online Audio	$14.99

FastTrack Ukulele

by Chad Johnson

Level 1

00114417	Method Book/Online Audio	$7.99
00158671	Songbook/Online Audio	$12.99

Level 2

00275508	Method Book/Online Audio	$9.99

FastTrack Violin

by Patrick Clark

Level 1

00141262	Method Book/Online Audio	$7.99

HAL•LEONARD®

Visit Hal Leonard online at **www.halleonard.com**

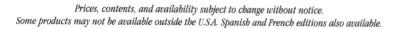